FLOWER FI

By MAY THEILGAARD WATTS

A KEY to SPRING WILD FLOWERS and FLOWER FAMILIES
East of the Rockies and North of the Smokies,
Exclusive of Trees and Shrubs.

© Nature Study Guild 1955

NATURE STUDY GUILD PUBLISHERS
A division of Keen Communications, Birmingham, AL

BOTANICAL TERMS USED IN DESCRIBING FLOWERS

①

anther — pollen-bearing part of stamen

calyx — outer part of flower, composed of sepals, usually green

corolla — part of flower between calyx and stamens, composed of petals

filament — stem of stamen

head — compact mass of small stemless flowers

Involucre — leafy growth encircling head or cluster

Irregular (flower) — having petals of different sizes and shapes

ovary — lower, enlarged part of pistil

inferior (ovary) — ovary united with the calyx

superior (ovary) — ovary having calyx and corolla inserted at its base

petal — one division of corolla

pistil — seed-bearing central part of flower

polypetalous — having separate petals

regular — having petals all of about same size and shape

sepal — one division of calyx

stamen — pollen-bearing part, composed of anther and filament

stigma — sticky part of pistil which receives pollen

style — neck of pistil, between stigma and ovary

sympetalous — having petals more or less united (one cannot be removed without tearing others)

umbel — cluster with stems arising from one point

alternate — coming out singly along stem

basal — growing on the ground at foot of plant

compound — made up of leaflets

entire — margin without teeth or lobes

leaflet — leaf-like part of a compound leaf

lobed — with deeply indented margin

net-veined — veins branching from midrib

opposite — having two leaves coming at same level

palmately compound — having leaflets coming from one point

parallel veins — veins running side by side from base to tip of leaf

perfoliate — having base surrounding stem

pinnately compound — having leaflets not all from one point

pubescent — covered with soft hair

sessile — without a stem

simple — not made up of leaflets

stipule — small leaf-like growth at base of stem

toothed — margin with edge like a saw

whorled — having several leaves from one level on stem

1. Start at the beginning (below).
2. Choose the description that fits the flower to be identified.
3. Proceed to the symbol indicated, on the page indicated.
4. Continue in this manner through the key until the flower is located in its family.
5. Continue within the family to the name and picture of your flower.

If the flowering part is composed of a modified leaf surrounding a spike bearing tiny flowers Go on page 4 to the **ARUM FAMILY**

If what looks like a flower is a mass of tightly-packed, stemless, small flowers with 2-parted stigmas; and this mass is surrounded by a green, leafy growth Go on page 58 to the **COMPOSITE FAMILY**

If flowers are not on a club-like spike nor in a compact head Go on page 5 to

START HERE

The ARUM FAMILY (Araceae)

Flowers inconspicuous, on a club-like spike (spadix), enfolded by a modified leaf (spathe), usually in moist, shady places.

If leaves are simple

—spathe white

It is **WILD CALLA**
Calla palustris

—spathe beef-colored

It is **SKUNK CABBAGE**
Symplocarpus foetidus

If leaves are compound

Go below to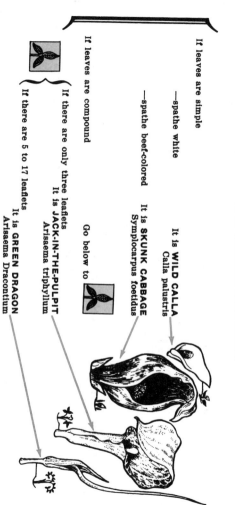

If there are only three leaflets
It is **JACK-IN-THE-PULPIT**
Arisaema triphyllum

If there are 5 to 17 leaflets
It is **GREEN DRAGON**
Arisaema Dracontium

If the leaves are parallel-veined, flowers usually three-parted
Go below to

If the leaves are net-veined, flowers usually five, or four-parted
Go on page 14 to

If the ovary is superior
Go below to

If the ovary is inferior
Go on page 11 to

If the stems are jointed, leaf bases sheathing, flowers seeming to melt
Go below to **SPIDERWORT FAMILY**

If the stems are not jointed
Go on page 6 to the **LILY FAMILY**

The SPIDERWORT FAMILY (Commelinaceae)

Stems jointed; leaf bases sheathing; petals ephemeral, often blue.

Leaves keeled, flowers blue, filaments bearded, juice mucilaginous

It is **SPIDERWORT**
Tradescantia virginiana

The LILY FAMILY (Liliaceae)

Flower parts in threes; stamens six; leaves parallel-veined; ovary superior, 3-celled.

If the sepals and petals are different in color

Go below to

If the sepals and petals are of the same color

Go on page 7 to

—petals red or purple

   It is **WAKE ROBIN**
   (**PRAIRIE TRILLIUM**)
      Trillium recurvatum

—petals white on plants not more than 6" high, blooming very early
   It is **DWARF TRILLIUM**
   (**PRAIRIE TRILLIUM**)
      Trillium nivale

—petals white, plants taller
  —flowers inverted
   It is **SHY TRILLIUM**
      Trillium flexipes

  —flowers upright
    —without purple stripes
     It is **WHITE TRILLIUM**
       Trillium grandiflorum

    —with purple stripes at base
     It is **PAINTED TRILLIUM**
       Trillium undulatum

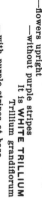

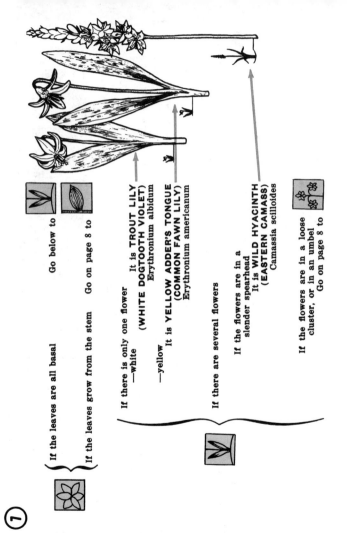

If the leaves are all basal Go below to

If the leaves grow from the stem Go on page 8 to

If there is only one flower

—white It is **TROUT LILY**
(**WHITE DOGTOOTH VIOLET**)
Erythronium albidum

—yellow It is **YELLOW ADDER'S TONGUE**
(**COMMON FAWN LILY**)
Erythronium americanum

If there are several flowers

If the flowers are in a
slender spearhead
It is **WILD HYACINTH**
(**EASTERN CAMASS**)
Camassia scilloides

If the flowers are in a loose
cluster, or in an umbel
Go on page 8 to

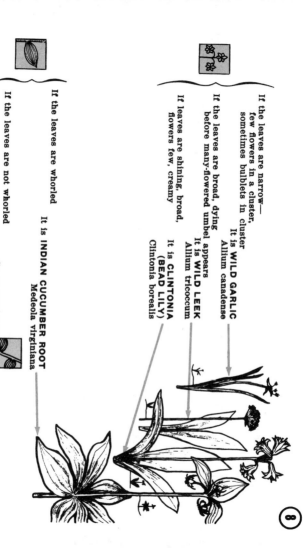

If the leaves are narrow—
few flowers in a cluster,
sometimes bulblets in cluster

It is **WILD GARLIC**
Allium canadense

If the leaves are broad, dying
before many-flowered umbel appears

It is **WILD LEEK**
Allium tricoccum

If leaves are shining, broad,
flowers few, creamy

It is **CLINTONIA
(BEAD LILY)**
Clintonia borealis

If the leaves are whorled

It is **INDIAN CUCUMBER ROOT**
Medeola virginiana

If the leaves are not whorled

Go on page 9 to

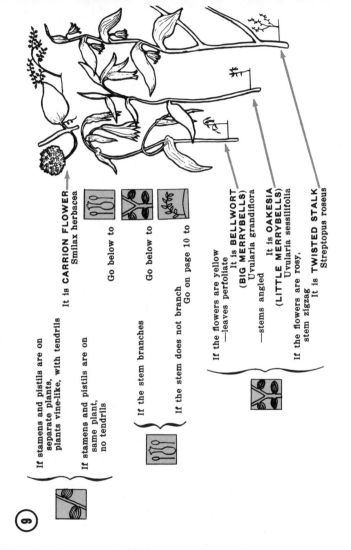

If stamens and pistils are on
separate plants,
plants vine-like, with tendrils

It is **CARRION FLOWER**
Smilax herbacea

If stamens and pistils are on
same plant,
no tendrils

If the stem branches

Go below to

If the stem does not branch
Go on page 10 to

If the flowers are yellow
—leaves perfoliate

It is **BELLWORT**
(**BIG MERRYBELLS**)
Uvularia grandiflora

—stems angled   It is **OAKESIA**
(**LITTLE MERRYBELLS**)
Uvularia sessilifolia

If the flowers are rosy,
stem zigzag

It is **TWISTED STALK**
Streptopus roseus

If the flowers are clustered at the end
of the stalk Go below to

If the flowers grow from place where
leaf joins stem Go below to

If flowers are 4-parted, leaf
bases heart-shaped
It is **WILD LILY-OF-THE-VALLEY**
(CANADA MAYFLOWER)
Maianthemum canadense

If the flowers are 6-parted

—flower cluster not branching
It is **STARRY SOLOMON PLUME**
(FALSE SOLOMON SEAL)
Smilacina stellata

—flower cluster branching
It is **FEATHERY SOLOMON PLUME**
(FALSE SPIKENARD)
Smilacina racemosa

If the leaves are flat, stem slender,
usually 2 flowers from place
where leaf joins stem
It is **SMALL SOLOMON SEAL**
Polygonatum biforum

If the leaves are ruffled, stem stout,
and there are usually several flowers
in a cluster from place where leaf
joins stem

It is **GREAT SOLOMON SEAL**
Polygonatum canaliculatum

⑩

 If the flowers are regular   Go below to

 If the flowers are irregular
    Go on page 12 to the ORCHID FAMILY

If the leaves are all basal, stamens 6
    Go below to the AMARYLLIS FAMILY

If the leaves are overlapping,
    stamens only 3
        Go below to the IRIS FAMILY

The AMARYLLIS FAMILY (Amaryllidaceae)

Ovary inferior; stamens 6, opening toward pistil.

If flowers are yellow, leaves grass-like

    It is **STAR GRASS**
    Hypoxis hirsuta

The IRIS FAMILY (Iridaceae)

Ovary inferior; stamens 3, opening away from pistil.

If the flowers are blue,
—sepals and petals alike

    It is **BLUE-EYED GRASS**
    Sisyrinchium angustifolium

—sepals and petals not alike

    It is **BLUE FLAG**
    Iris versicolor

The ORCHID FAMILY (Orchidaceae)

Flowers irregular, with one petal forming a lip or pouch; stamens 1 or 2; pollen usually in sticky mass; seeds tiny, numerous.

If the lip is a pouch   Go on page 13 to

If the lip is spreading   Go below to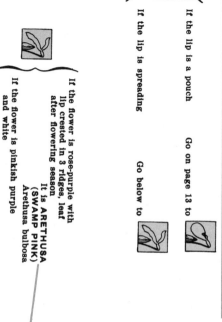

If the flower is rose-purple with
lip crested in 3 ridges, leaf
after flowering season
    It is **ARETHUSA**
    (SWAMP PINK)
    Arethusa bulbosa

If the flower is pinkish purple
and white
        It is **SHOWY ORCHIS**
        Orchis spectabilis

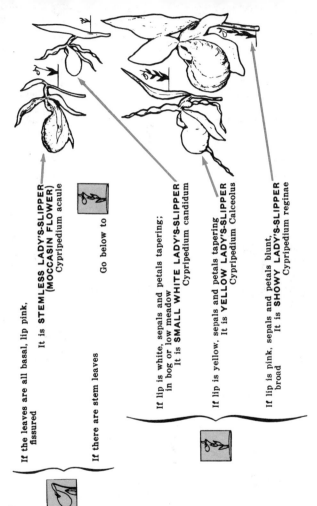

If the leaves are all basal, lip pink, fissured

It is **STEMLESS LADY'S-SLIPPER**
(MOCCASIN FLOWER)
Cypripedium acaule

If there are stem leaves   Go below to

If lip is white, sepals and petals tapering;
in bog or low meadow
It is **SMALL WHITE LADY'S-SLIPPER**
Cypripedium candidum

If lip is yellow, sepals and petals tapering
It is **YELLOW LADY'S-SLIPPER**
Cypripedium Calceolus

If lip is pink, sepals and petals blunt,
broad   It is **SHOWY LADY'S-SLIPPER**
Cypripedium reginae

If the flowers have numerous stamens (usually more than 12)

Go below to

If the flowers have few stamens (rarely more than twice as many as petals or sepals)

Go on page 22 to

If the stamens are united by their filaments into a sheath around the pistil, the whole forming a club-like center

Go on page 20 to the
MALLOW FAMILY

If stamens are not united

If the sepals are united at the base, and petals and stamens are attached to calyx tube

Go on page 21 to the
ROSE FAMILY

If the sepals are not united; and stamens, sepals, petals, and pistil (or pistils) are, all unconnected

Go on page 15 to

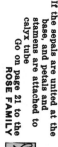 

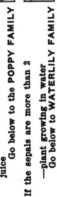

If there are several pistils
Go on page 16 to the BUTTERCUP FAMILY

If there is only one pistil   Go below to

If sepals are 2, falling off when flower
opens, petals in 4s, milky or colored
juice
    Go below to the POPPY FAMILY

If the sepals are more than 2

  —plant growing in water
    Go below to WATERLILY FAMILY

  —plant not in water
    Go on page 17 to BANEBERRY

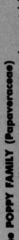

The POPPY FAMILY (Papaveraceae)
Petals 4 to 12; stamens numerous; seeds many; juice
colored or milky.

If flower is yellow with 4 petals

It is CELANDINE POPPY
Stylophorum diphyllum
It is BLOODROOT
Sanguinaria canadensis

If flower is white, 8 or 12 petals,

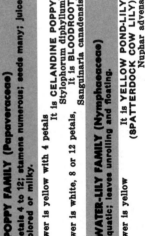

The WATER-LILY FAMILY (Nymphaeaceae)
Aquatic; leaves unrolling and floating.

If flower is yellow

It is YELLOW POND-LILY
(SPATTERDOCK COW LILY)
Nuphar advena

If flower is white

It is FRAGRANT WATER-LILY
Nymphaea odorata

The BUTTERCUP or CROWFOOT FAMILY (Ranunculaceae)

Stamens numerous; pistils usually several; leaves often deeply divided, and dilated at base.

If the flower has no corolla, but a colored, or white, calyx that looks like a corolla (Where only one of these two rows is present it is called the calyx)
Go on page 19 to

If both the calyx and corolla are present
Go below to

If the leaves are all basal
—leaves 3-lobed

—leaves 3-parted, yellow root

—leaves deeply divided, silky, hairy

It is HEPATICA
Hepatica acutiloba

It is GOLDTHREAD
Coptis groenlandica

It is PASQUE FLOWER
Anemone patens

If there are stem leaves
Go below to

Stamens and pistils on same plant
Go on page 17 to

Stamens and pistils on separate plants
EARLY MEADOW RUE
Thalictrum dioicum

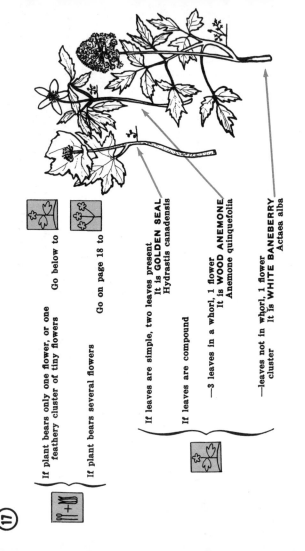

If plant bears only one flower, or one
feathery cluster of tiny flowers   Go below to

If plant bears several flowers

Go on page 18 to

If leaves are simple, two leaves present
It is **GOLDEN SEAL**
Hydrastis canadensis

If leaves are compound

—3 leaves in a whorl, 1 flower
It is **WOOD ANEMONE**
Anemone quinquefolia

—leaves not in whorl, 1 flower
cluster   It is **WHITE BANEBERRY**
Actaea alba

If flowers are white

— plants low, in woods

— flowers in a cluster surrounded by a whorl of leaves
It is **RUE ANEMONE**
Anemonella thalictroides

— flowers borne at various levels along the stem
It is **FALSE RUE ANEMONE**
Isopyrum biternatum

— plants more than 1 foot tall, not in woods

— upper leaves sessile
It is **PRAIRIE ANEMONE**
Anemone canadensis

— upper leaves with stems
It is **THIMBLEWEED**
Anemone virginiana

If flowers are yellow
It is **MARSH MARIGOLD**
Caltha palustris

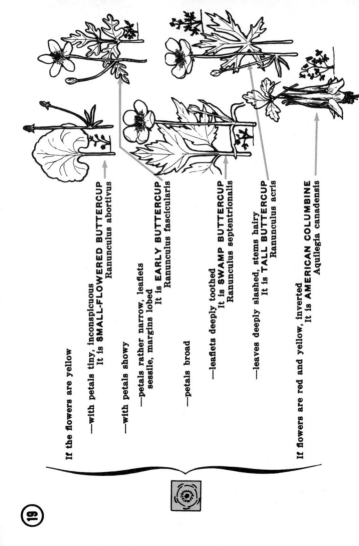

If the flowers are yellow

—with petals tiny, inconspicuous
It is **SMALL-FLOWERED BUTTERCUP**
Ranunculus abortivus

—with petals showy

—petals rather narrow, leaflets
sessile, margins lobed
It is **EARLY BUTTERCUP**
Ranunculus fascicularis

—petals broad

—leaflets deeply toothed
It is **SWAMP BUTTERCUP**
Ranunculus septentrionalis

—leaves deeply slashed, stems hairy
It is **TALL BUTTERCUP**
Ranunculus acris

If flowers are red and yellow, inverted
It is **AMERICAN COLUMBINE**
Aquilegia canadensis

The MALLOW FAMILY (Malvaceae)

Flowers with a club-like center composed of pistil, surrounded by column of stamens united by their filaments; buds rolled; leaves palmately-veined.

If leaves are round
petals notched, white or pinkish;
fruit round with cheese-like form
It is **COMMON MALLOW** or **CHEESES**
Malva rotundifolia.

If the leaves are deeply cut,
stem hairy, flowers magenta
It is **POPPY MALLOW**
Callirhoe involucrata

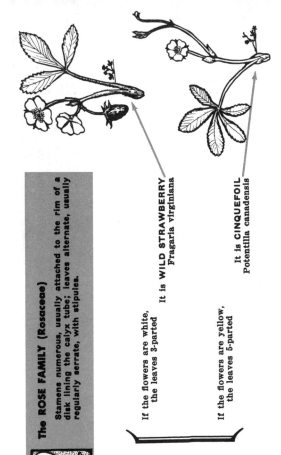

The ROSE FAMILY (Rosaceae)

Stamens numerous, usually attached to the rim of a disk lining the calyx tube; leaves alternate, usually regularly serrate, with stipules.

If the flowers are white, the leaves 3-parted

It is **WILD STRAWBERRY**
Fragaria virginiana

If the flowers are yellow, the leaves 5-parted

It is **CINQUEFOIL**
Potentilla canadensis

If the flowers are polypetalous (one petal may be pulled off without tearing any others)

Go below to

If the flowers are sympetalous (petals joined along their sides)

Go on page 45 to

If the flower is 4-parted or 2-parted

Go on page 23 to

If the flower is 5-parted

Go on page 27 to

If the flower is 6 to 9 parted with 6 to 9 stamens opposite the petals; stamens opening by hinges at top

Go on page 23 to **BARBERRY FAMILY**

If the flower is 3-parted, without petals, sepals 3, mahogany-colored, united with ovary, stamens 6 or 12

It is **WILD GINGER**
Asarum canadense
(BIRTHWORT FAMILY, Aristolochaceae)

The BARBERRY FAMILY (Berberidaceae)

Petals 6 to 9; stamens usually same number as petals and opposite them; anthers usually opening by hinged valve at top.

If the leaves are all basal — It is TWINLEAF
Jeffersonia diphylla

If there are stem leaves

—two leaves only — It is MAY APPLE
Podophyllum peltatum

—many small leaves — It is BLUE COHOSH
Caulophyllum thalictroides

If the flowers are regular

—tiny tightly-clustered, surrounded by 4 showy bracts, ovary inferior
Go on page 44 to
DOGWOOD FAMILY

—flowers loosely-clustered, 6 stamens
Go on page 25 to
MUSTARD FAMILY

Go on page 24 to
FUMITORY FAMILY

23

The FUMITORY FAMILY (Fumarioideae)
(or sub-family of Papaveraceae)

Flowers pendent, flattened, sac-like, with petals separate or slightly united; leaves fern-like.

If the leaves are not all basal; flower 1-petaled, not heart-shaped

—flowers pink   It is **PALE CORYDALIS**
Corydalis sempervirens

—flowers yellow   It is **GOLDEN CORYDALIS**
Corydalis aurea

If the leaves are all basal, the flowers heart-shaped

—with rounded spurs   It is **SQUIRREL CORN**
Dicentra canadensis

—with pointed spurs   It is **DUTCHMAN'S BREECHES**
Dicentra Cucullaria

The MUSTARD FAMILY (Cruciferae)

Juice pungent; flower with 4 petals, 4 sepals, and 6 stamens (4 long, 2 short); fruit 2-parted with thin partition.

If flowers are yellow   Go below to

If flowers are white or rose purple
                          Go on page 26 to

 It is **FIELD MUSTARD (CHARLOCK)**
Brassica Kaber

If flower is more than ½ inch across, leaves not deeply-lobed

If flower is less than ½ inch across, leaves deeply-lobed

— leaf margin toothed   It is **BLACK MUSTARD**
Brassica nigra

— leaf margin not toothed   It is **YELLOW ROCKET**
Barbarea vulgaris

If there are 3 leaves, deeply-divided, in a whorl
It is **TOOTHWORT**
Dentaria laciniata

If leaves are simple, not whorled

—flowers less than ½ inch

—pods triangular, flowers tiny
It is **SHEPHERD'S PURSE**
Capsella Bursa-Pastoris

—pods oval, flowers tiny
It is **PEPPERGRASS**
Lepidium virginicum

—pods long
It is **ROCK CRESS**
Arabis lyrata

—flowers ½ inch broad, fruit long

—white-flowered, smooth It is **SPRING CRESS**
(**BULB BITTER CRESS**)
Cardamine bulbosa

—rose-purple, pubescent It is **SPRING CRESS**
(**DOUGLAS BITTER CRESS**)
Cardamine Douglassii

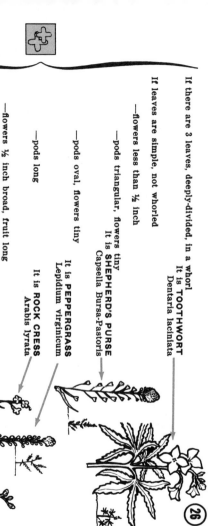

If the flower is regular
(having petals all of the same size and shape)
Go below to

If the flower is irregular
(having petals of different shapes)
Go on page 32 to

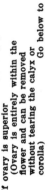

If ovary is superior
(Ovary is entirely within the
flower and can be removed
without tearing the calyx or
corolla)
Go below to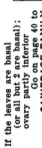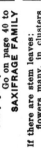

If ovary is not superior
Go below to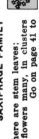

If the leaves are simple
Go on page 28 to

If the leaves are compound
Go on page 39 to
OXALIS FAMILY

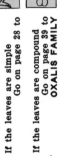

If the leaves are basal
(or all but 2 are basal);
ovary partly inferior
Go on page 40 to
SAXIFRAGE FAMILY

If there are stem leaves;
flowers many, in clusters
Go on page 41 to

If flowers have 5 sepals

Go on page 29 to

If flowers have 2 sepals, fleshy leaves
Go below to PORTULACA FAMILY

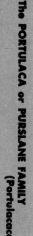

The PORTULACA or PURSLANE FAMILY (Portulacaceae)

Leaves succulent; flowers open only in sunshine; stamens usually 5 and opposite petals; 2 sepals.

If the leaves are narrow, grass-like

It is **SPRING BEAUTY**
Claytonia virginica

If the leaves are entire;
joints of stem swollen
Go on page 30 to PINK FAMILY

If the leaves are deeply-lobed
Go below to GERANIUM FAMILY

The GERANIUM FAMILY (Geraniaceae)

Leaves deeply-lobed; stems soft; stamens 10; styles 5-parted.

If flower is 1" or more across;
leaves somewhat circular in outline;
stem usually unbranched   It is **WILD GERANIUM
(CRANESBILL)**
Geranium maculatum

If flower is ½" or less across; stems much branched

—flowers in a close cluster
It is **CAROLINA CRANESBILL**
Geranium carolinianum

—flowers not in close clusters;
stems ruddy; with strong odor
It is **HERB ROBERT**
Geranium Robertianum

The PINK FAMILY (Caryophyllaceae)

Leaves opposite, entire, often united at base; stems usually swollen at joints; sepals 5; styles 2 to 5.

If the sepals are separate or nearly so
Go below to

If the sepals are united into a tube or cup
Go on page 31 to

If the petals are not notched, or only slightly notched
—with petals longer than sepals
It is **BLUNT-LEAVED SANDWORT**
Arenaria lateriflora.

—with sepals longer than petals
It is **THYME-LEAVED SANDWORT**
Arenaria serpyllifolia.

If petals are deeply cleft
—sepals longer than petals
It is **CHICKWEED**
Stellaria media.

—sepals shorter, plant very hairy
It is **MOUSE-EAR CHICKWEED**
Cerastium vulgatum

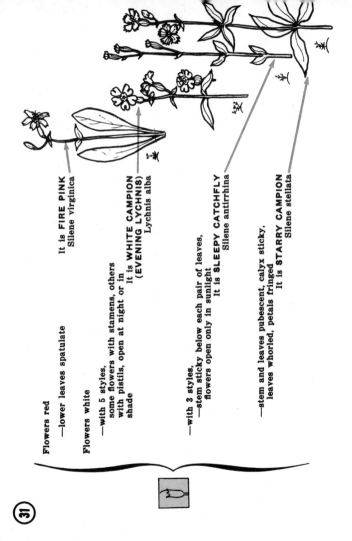

Flowers red

—lower leaves spatulate

It is **FIRE PINK**
Silene virginica

Flowers white

—with 5 styles,
some flowers with stamens, others
with pistils, open at night or in
shade

It is **WHITE CAMPION
(EVENING LYCHNIS)**
Lychnis alba

—with 3 styles,
—stem sticky below each pair of leaves,
flowers open only in sunlight

It is **SLEEPY CATCHFLY**
Silene antirrhina

—stem and leaves pubescent, calyx sticky,
leaves whorled, petals fringed

It is **STARRY CAMPION**
Silene stellata

If the colored parts of the flower are 3, stamens united to each other and to petals
Go on page 33 to **MILKWORT FAMILY**

If there are 5 petals

Go below to

If there are 5 stamens; the lower petal marked with lines
Go on page 34 to **VIOLET FAMILY**

If there are 10 stamens; 2 petals forming a keel
Go on page 36 to **LEGUME FAMILY**

The MILKWORT FAMILY (Polygalaceae)

Flowers irregular with 5 sepals, 2 of them large and petal-like; 3 petals, somewhat united to each other and to stamens.

If the flower is rose-purple
  with a fringe at the tip; leaves
  broad, leathery, small on lower
  part of stem   It is **FRINGED POLYGALA**
                              Polygala paucifolia

If flower is white
  small, on a spike; usually on rocky
  soil   It is **SENECA SNAKEROOT**
                              Polygala Senega

The VIOLET FAMILY (Violaceae)

Flowers irregular with lowest petal enlarged and spurred; stamens joined around ovary; seed-capsules 3-parted; leaves with stipules.

If the leaves are all basal   Go below to

If the leaves are not all basal   Go below to

If the flower is yellow

    stems downy,   It is **DOWNY YELLOW VIOLET**
                                       Viola pubescens

    stems smooth,   It is **SMOOTH YELLOW VIOLET**
                                         Viola pensylvanica

If the flower is white, bearded—
    rosy on underside,   It is **CANADA VIOLET**
                                         Viola canadensis

If the flower is white, beardless
    —with ovate leaves; reddish-stemmed;
        purple-veined   It is **SWEET WHITE VIOLET**
                                         Viola blanda

    —with lance-shaped leaves
        It is **LANCE-LEAVED VIOLET**
                                         Viola lanceolata

If the flower is blue to violet   Go on page 35 to

(34)

If leaves are entire   Go below to

If leaves are deeply-lobed   Go below to

If leaves are heart-shaped

  —stems and leaves smooth
    —with beards on side petals knobbed;
      flowers overtopping leaves
        It is **MARSH BLUE VIOLET**
           Viola cucullata

    —with beards not knobbed;
      flowers seldom overtopping leaves
        It is **COMMON VIOLET**
           Viola papilionacea
        Grayish-white form is
        CONFEDERATE VIOLET

  —stems and under-parts of leaves
    hairy   It is **HAIRY BLUE VIOLET**
           Viola sororia

If leaves are arrow-shaped
    It is **ARROW-LEAVED VIOLET**
        Viola sagittata

If leaves are lobed less than half way
    to mid-vein; side petals bearded
      It is **PALMATE VIOLET**
        Viola palmata

If leaves are cleft almost to mid-vein;
    no petals bearded
      It is **BIRDSFOOT VIOLET**
        Viola pedata

The LEGUME or PULSE FAMILY (Leguminosae)

Flower usually irregular, the 2 lower petals forming a keel enclosing pistil and 10 stamens; leaves usually compound with stipules; fruit a pod.

If the leaves have 3 leaflets,
—with end leaflet stalked   Go below to

—with end leaflet not stalked
     Go on page 37 to

If the leaves have more than 3 leaflets,
     Go on page 38 to

If the plant is procumbent, 6" high; flowers yellow, in a head
     It is **BLACK MEDIC**
     Medicago lupulina

If plant is upright, 1 to 4 ft. high
—with purple flowers
     It is **ALFALFA**
     Medicago sativa

—with white flowers; 5 ft. tall or more
     It is **WHITE MELILOT**
     (WHITE SWEET CLOVER)
     Melilotus alba

—with yellow flowers; shorter (3 ft.),
     It is **YELLOW MELILOT**
     (YELLOW SWEET CLOVER)
     Melilotus officinalis

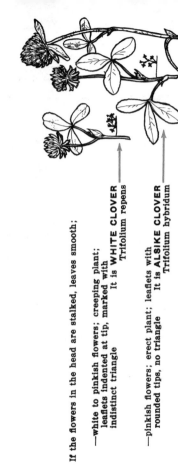

If the flowers in the head are stalked, leaves smooth;

—white to pinkish flowers; creeping plant;
leaflets indented at tip, marked with
indistinct triangle   It is **WHITE CLOVER**
Trifolium repens

—pinkish flowers; erect plant; leaflets with
rounded tips, no triangle   It is **ALSIKE CLOVER**
Trifolium hybridum

If the flowers in the head are sessile, roseate;
leaves hairy; distinct triangle   It is **RED CLOVER**
Trifolium pratense

If leaves are palmately-compound

It is **LUPINE**
Lupinus perennis

If leaves are pinnately-compound, tipped with
tendrils; plants trailing or climbing

Go below to

If leaves are thick, prominently-
veined; back and side petals curved
upward; flowers purple

It is **WILD PEA**
Lathyrus venosus

If leaves are thin; side petals joined to keel
—plants smooth

—flowers 4 to 8, purple, ¾ in. long
It is **AMERICAN VETCH**
Vicia americana

—flowers 10 or more, pale tip of
keel bluish
It is **WOOD VETCH**
Vicia caroliniana

—plant hairy; flowers many,
flowers in mats; flowers many;
It is **HAIRY VETCH**
Vicia villosa

The OXALIS or WOOD-SORREL FAMILY
(Oxalidaceae)

Juice sour; leaves with 3 notched leaflets; pod cylindric.

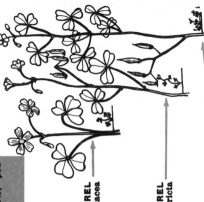

If flowers are violet, veined; leaves all basal   It is **VIOLET WOOD SORREL**
Oxalis violacea

If flowers are yellow; leaves from stem

—plant somewhat erect, hairy; stipules narrow, pale   It is **YELLOW WOOD SORREL**
Oxalis stricta

—plant creeping, rooting from stems, smooth, with dark, broad stipules   It is **CREEPING WOOD SORREL**
Oxalis corniculata

The SAXIFRAGE FAMILY (Saxifragaceae)

Ovary partly inferior, many-seeded; styles usually 2; leaves often all, or almost all, basal.

If the petals are deeply divided; and there are 2 stem leaves
It is MITERWORT (BISHOP'S CAP).
Mitella diphylla.

If petals are entire; and there are no stem leaves
Go below to

If the leaves are heart-shaped
—flower spikes not branched, flowers white
It is FOAM FLOWER
Tiarella cordifolia.

—flower spikes branched, flowers greenish
It is ALUM ROOT
Heuchera americana.

If leaves are oval or elongated
—petals white; leaves less than 3 inches;
It is EARLY SAXIFRAGE
Saxifraga virginiensis

—petals greenish; leaves 4 to 10 inches;
It is SWAMP SAXIFRAGE
Saxifraga pensylvanica.
sepals reflexed
sepals erect

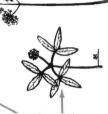

If there are only 3 leaves made up
of 5 leaflets; and the 3 leaves arise
from one point; leaflets not lobed;
fruit red, juicy   Go below to GINSENG FAMILY

If leaves are not from one point;
stems usually hollow; strong-odored;
leaves usually deeply-divided; 2 styles;
fruit dry, 2-parted
Go on page 42 to PARSLEY FAMILY

The GINSENG FAMILY (Araliaceae)

Flowers in umbels; fruit a drupe; leaves often compound, whorled.

If there is a single whorl of leaves;
fruit red; one umbel

—leaflets up to 4" long, pointed,
It is COMMON GINSENG
Panax quinquefolius

—leaflets 1" to 2" long, blunt, sessile,
It is DWARF GINSENG
Panax trifolius

If the umbels are on a naked stalk with
a single compound leaf rising from the
ground; fruit purplish-black
It is WILD SARSAPARILLA
Aralia nudicaulis

The PARSLEY FAMILY (Umbelliferae)

Flowers in umbels; styles 2, ovary inferior; leaves usually compound with sheathing bases.

If flowers are yellow   Go below to

If flowers are white   Go on page 43 to

If leaves are composed of 3 main divisions
                Go below to

If leaves have more than 3 main divisions
                It is **WILD PARSNIP**
                  Pastinaca sativa

If leaf margins are toothed; center flower
of each cluster without a stalk
          It is **GOLDEN ALEXANDERS**
                 Zizea aurea

If leaf margins are entire
           It is **TAENIDIA**
           (**YELLOW PIMPERNEL**)
           Taenidia integerrima

WHITE

If plant is very small; blooming in early
spring; with leaves finely-divided
Go below to

If plant is about 2 feet tall; not blooming in
very early spring; flower head small,
inconspicuous   Go below to

If plant is 3 to 8 feet; umbels 4 to 12 in. across;
stems grooved
Go on page 44 to

If flowers are on naked or nearly
naked stem; anthers red-brown
It is **HARBINGER OF SPRING**
Erigenia bulbosa.

If flowers are on a leafy stem; leaves
light green   It is **CHERVIL**
Chaerophyllum procumbens

If leaves are composed of 3 leaflets;
petals turned in at the tips
It is **HONEWORT**
Cryptotaenia canadensis

If leaves are composed of many leaflets

—plant smooth, licorice-flavored
It is **SMOOTH SWEET CICELY**
(**ANISE ROOT**)
Osmorhiza longistylis

—plant hairy, not licorice-flavored
It is **HAIRY SWEET CICELY**
Osmorhiza Claytoni

If plant has hairy stems and broad irregularly-toothed leaflets; umbels 8 to 12" across

It is **COW PARSNIP**
Heracleum maximum

If plant has purple, hollow, smooth stems, and finely-toothed, oval to oblong leaflets

It is **ANGELICA**
Angelica atropurpurea

The DOGWOOD FAMILY (Cornaceae)

Flowers tightly packed in a head surrounded by 4 showy, petal-like leaves, (bracts)

Low herb with white bracts

It is **BUNCHBERRY**
Cornus canadensis

If the flowers are stemless and crowded into a compact head surrounded by a leafy involucre Go on page 58 to **COMPOSITE FAMILY**

Go below to

If each flower has its own stem (however short)

If leaves are leathery, stamens 8 to 10 Go on page 46 to **HEATH FAMILY**

Go below to

If leaves are not leathery, stamens 5 or less Go below to

If ovary is superior Go below to

If ovary is inferior Go on page 56 to

If flower is regular Go on page 47 to

If flower is irregular Go on page 53 to

The HEATH FAMILY (Ericaceae)

Plants usually woody (these are trailing); leaves often leathery; stamens twice as many as corolla lobes, and on edge of fleshy disk; stamens opening at tips.

If the flowers are not urn-shaped, about ½ inch across, very fragrant, pink; leaves and stems with coarse brown hairs, leaves heart-shaped at base

It is **TRAILING ARBUTUS**
Epigaea repens

If flowers are urn-shaped

Go below to

If leaves are clustered at top of warm-brown stem; flowers at bases of leaves, blooming into summer

It is **WINTERGREEN**
Gaultheria procumbens

If leaves are along stem; flowers at tip of growth

It is **BEARBERRY**
Arctostaphylos Uva-ursi

If leaf (or leaflets), margins are entire, Go below to

If leaf margins are toothed or lobed, Go on page 51 to

If style is 3-lobed, pod 3-celled, Go on page 48 to **POLEMONIUM FAMILY**

If style is simple, Go below to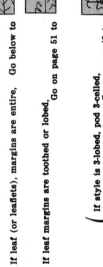

If ovary is deeply 4-lobed, stamens alternate with petals, Go on page 49 to **BORAGE FAMILY**

If ovary is one-celled, stamens opposite petals, Go on page 50 to **PRIMROSE FAMILY**

The POLEMONIUM or PHLOX FAMILY
(Polemoniaceae)

Style 3-lobed; pod 3-celled; stamens connected to corolla tube; leaves opposite or compound; flowers clustered.

If leaves are compound; flowers nodding, light blue-violet,

It is **JACOB'S LADDER**
Polemonium reptans

If leaves are simple,

Go below to

If the plant is on sandy soil; petals cleft half-way

It is **CLEFT PHLOX**
Phlox bifida

If plant is in open grassy woods or prairie; flowers pink-purple; hairy

It is **PRAIRIE PHLOX**
(DOWNY PHLOX)
Phlox pilosa

If plant is in woods; flowers lilac, violet, to white, fragrant

It is **WILD BLUE PHLOX**
(WILD SWEET WILLIAM)
Phlox divaricata

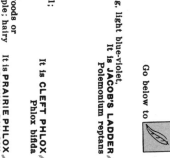

The BORAGE FAMILY (Boraginaceae)

Ovary 4-lobed; fruit 4 seed-like nutlets; flowers in an elongated, unrolling cluster.

If plant is smooth,
flowers blue (occasionally white)
It is **VIRGINIA COWSLIP**
Mertensia virginica

If plant is hairy,

—with blue flowers,
It is **FORGET-ME-NOT**
Myosotis scorpioides

—with orange flowers,
It is **HOARY PUCCOON**
Lithospermum canescens

—with deep garnet flowers,
It is **HOUND'S-TONGUE**
Cynoglossum officinale

The PRIMROSE FAMILY (Primulaceae)

Stamens opposite petals; fruit one-celled; leaves all at one level; main flower stem thick.

If leaves are in a whorl under 2 star-like white flowers,

It is **STAR FLOWER**
Trientalis borealis

If leaves are all basal, flower inverted, corolla turned back,

It is **SHOOTING STAR**
Dodecatheon Meadia

(50)

If styles are 2-cleft; stamens usually
loosely protruding
Go on page 52 to WATERLEAF FAMILY

If there is one style
Go below to NIGHTSHADE FAMILY

The NIGHTSHADE FAMILY (Solanaceae)

Flowers regular; stamens 5; petals 5; style and
stigma single; leaves rank-smelling; fruit often a
berry.

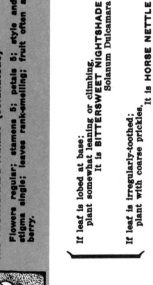

If leaf is lobed at base;
plant somewhat leaning or climbing,
It is BITTERSWEET NIGHTSHADE
Solanum Dulcamara

If leaf is irregularly-toothed;
plant with coarse prickles, it is HORSE NETTLE
Solanum carolinense

The WATERLEAF FAMILY (Hydrophyllaceae)

Styles 2; leaves usually deeply-divided and hairy;
flowers white to violet.

If the flowers are clustered; stamens
conspicuously protruding; plant one foot
high, or more.
       Go below to

If the flowers are not clustered;
stamens not protruding; plant less than
one foot high.
       It is ELLISIA
       Ellisia nyctelea

If plant is smooth; all leaves deeply-divided.
       It is VIRGINIA WATERLEAF
       Hydrophyllum virginianum

If plant is hairy; basal leaves deeply-divided,
but stem leaves 5-lobed; small appendages
between sepals
       It is APPENDAGED WATERLEAF
       Hydrophyllum appendiculatum

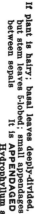

If flower is only very slightly sympetalous; flower pendent, sac-like,
Go on page 24 to **FUMITORY FAMILY**

If flower is two-lipped,   Go below to

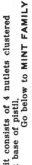

If fruit is 2-celled, many seeded,
Go on page 54 to **FIGWORT FAMILY (SNAPDRAGON FAMILY)**

If fruit consists of 4 nutlets clustered at base of pistil,
Go below to **MINT FAMILY**

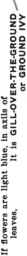

The MINT FAMILY (Labiatae)

Flowers 2-lipped; ovary 4-lobed; stigma 2-lobed; stems usually square; stamens 4 or 2.

If flowers are light blue, in axils of leaves,   It is **GILL-OVER-THE-GROUND** or **GROUND IVY**
Glechoma hederacea

If flowers are purplish, in spikes,   It is **SELF-HEAL**
Prunella vulgaris

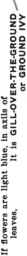

53

The FIGWORT FAMILY (Scrophulariaceae)

Corolla irregular, sympetalous; stamens of 2 lengths or only 2; style single; fruit a many seeded 2-cell capsule.

 If flowers are spurred,

Go below to

If flowers are not spurred,

Go below to

Flowers blue-violet, ½ in. long; plant very slender;

It is **OLDFIELD TOADFLAX**
Linaria canadensis

Flowers yellow and orange,

It is **BUTTER-AND-EGGS**
Linaria vulgaris

 Flower cluster short, heavy, flowers yellow and magenta,

It is **LOUSEWORT**
Pedicularis canadensis

Flowers in a loose cluster,

Go on page 55 to

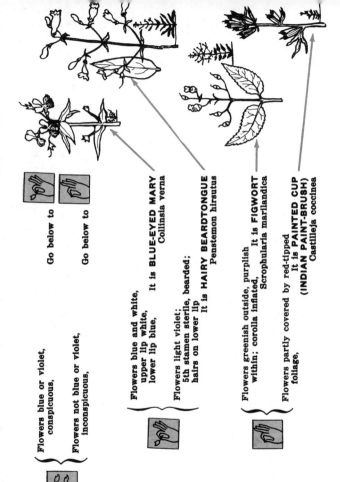

Flowers blue or violet,
conspicuous,

Go below to

Flowers not blue or violet,
inconspicuous,

Go below to

Flowers blue and white,
upper lip white,
lower lip blue,   It is **BLUE-EYED MARY**
Collinsia verna

Flowers light violet;
5th stamen sterile, bearded;
hairs on lower lip
It is **HAIRY BEARDTONGUE**
Penstemon hirsutus

Flowers greenish outside, purplish
within; corolla inflated,   It is **FIGWORT**
Scrophularia marilandica

Flowers partly covered by red-tipped
foliage,
It is **PAINTED CUP**
(INDIAN PAINT-BRUSH)
Castilleja coccinea

If flower is 4-parted, leaves in whorls, or connected by stipules,
Go below to **MADDER FAMILY**

If flower is 5-parted; leaves opposite,
Go on page 57 to **HONEYSUCKLE FAMILY**

The MADDER FAMILY (Rubiaceae)

Flowers 4-parted; leaves in whorls, or connected by stipules.

If leaves are not in whorls,
—flowers paired, white
It is **PARTRIDGE BERRY**
Mitchella repens
—flowers not paired, blue
It is **BLUET**
Houstonia caerulea

If leaves are in whorls of six, stems square
—stems smooth, flowers from tips of stems,
It is **SHINY BEDSTRAW**
Galium concinnum
—stems bristly, flowers from axil of leaves,
It is **CATCHWEED BEDSTRAW**
Galium Aparine

If leaves are in whorls of four,
—smooth, several-veined,
It is **NORTHERN BEDSTRAW**
Galium boreale
—hairy, one-veined,
It is **HAIRY BEDSTRAW**
Galium pilosum

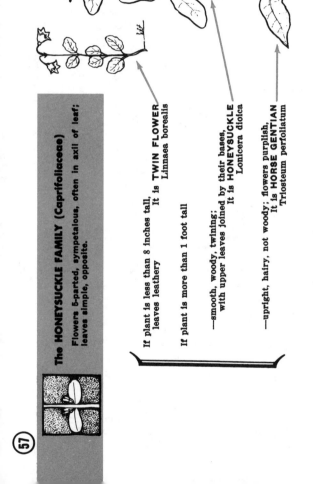

The HONEYSUCKLE FAMILY (Caprifoliaceae)

Flowers 5-parted, sympetalous, often in axil of leaf; leaves simple, opposite.

If plant is less than 8 inches tall, leaves leathery It is **TWIN FLOWER**
    Linnaea borealis

If plant is more than 1 foot tall

—smooth, woody, twining; with upper leaves joined by their bases, It is **HONEYSUCKLE**
    Lonicera dioica

—upright, hairy, not woody; flowers purplish, It is **HORSE GENTIAN**
    Triosteum perfoliatum

The COMPOSITE FAMILY (Compositae)

Flowers packed into heads, surrounded by leafy involucre; anthers united to form a tube around style; style 2-cleft at tip.

If the flowers are of 2 kinds: tubular at center, closed-fan shape on outside,

Go below to

If flowers are all closed-fan shape,

Go on page 59 to

If flowers are all tubular; plant white-woolly,

Go below to

with small basal leaves,

It is EVERLASTING
Antennaria canadensis

with broad basal leaves,

It is PLANTAIN-LEAVED
EVERLASTING
Antennaria plantaginifolia

Flowers all yellow,

It is GOLDEN RAGWORT
Senecio aureus

Flowers not all yellow,

Go on page 59 to

If ray flowers are yellow,
disc flowers purplish-brown
It is **BROWN-EYED SUSAN**
Rudbeckia hirta

If flowers are not yellow,

ray flowers pinkish to violet, numerous, crowded

—flowers blue-violet,
It is **ROBIN'S PLANTAIN**
Erigeron pulchellus

—flowers rose violet,
It is **COMMON FLEABANE**
Erigeron philadelphicus

ray flowers white, not numerous or crowded,
It is **OX-EYE DAISY**
Chrysanthemum Leucanthemum

If there is only one head on a stalk   Go on page 60 to

If there are several heads on a stalk,
Go on page 60 to

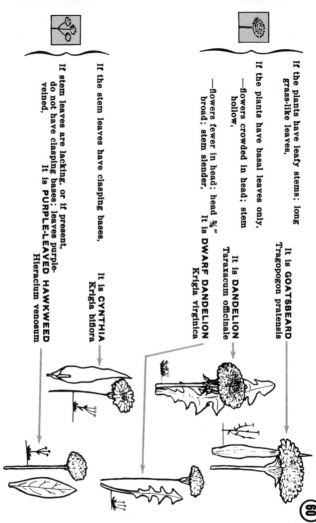

If the plants have leafy stems; long grass-like leaves,

It is **GOATSBEARD**
Tragopogon pratensis

If the plants have basal leaves only,

—flowers crowded in head; stem hollow,

—flowers fewer in head; head ¾" broad; stem slender,

It is **DANDELION**
Taraxacum officinale

It is **DWARF DANDELION**
Krigia virginica

If the stem leaves have clasping bases,

It is **CYNTHIA**
Krigia biflora

If stem leaves are lacking, or if present, do not have clasping bases; leaves purple-veined,

It is **PURPLE-LEAVED HAWKWEED**
Hieracium venosum

INDEX
to
COMMON NAMES
and
FAMILIES

Other books in the pocket-sized "finder" series:

for U.S. and Canada east of the Rockies
- **TREE FINDER** - native and common introduced trees
- **FLOWER FINDER** - spring wildflowers & flower families
- **WINTER TREE FINDER** - leafless winter trees
- **FERN FINDER** - native ferns of the Midwest and Northeast
- **BERRY FINDER** - native plants with fleshy fruits
- **TRACK FINDER** - tracks and footprints of mammals
- **LIFE ON INTERTIDAL ROCKS** - organisms of North Atlantic coast
- **WINTER WEED FINDER** - dry plant structures in winter

for the Pacific Coast
- **PACIFIC COAST TREE FINDER** - native trees, Sitka to San Diego
- **REDWOOD REGION FLOWER FINDER** - wildflowers of the coastal fog belt
- **PACIFIC COAST MAMMALS** - mammals, their tracks, other signs

for Rocky Mtn. and desert states
- **ROCKY MOUNTAIN TREE FINDER** - native Rocky Mountain trees
- **ROCKY MOUNTAIN FLOWER FINDER** - wildflowers below tree line
- **MOUNTAIN STATE MAMMALS** - mammals, their tracks, skulls, and scat

for Stargazers
- **CONSTELLATION FINDER** - patterns in the night sky and star stories

NATURE STUDY GUIDES are published by KEEN COMMUNICATIONS, PO Box 43673, Birmingham, AL 35243 (888) 604-4537, naturestudy.com. SEE keencommunication.com for our full line of outdoor activity guides by MENASHA RIDGE PRESS and WILDERNESS PRESS. Including regional and national parks hiking, camping, backpacking, and more.